F. Jay Haynes
Photographer

Montana Historical Society

This book is dedicated to
Isabel M. Haynes
and in memory of Jack Ellis Haynes

Library of Congress Cataloging in Publication Data
Main entry under title:
F. Jay Haynes, photographer
  1. West (U.S.) — Description and travel — Views.
2. West (U.S.) — History — 1848-1950 — Pictorial works.
3. Haynes, F. Jay (Frank Jay), 1853-1921. I. Montana
Historical Society.
F595.F13   770'.92'4   81-6712
ISBN 0-917298-04-7   AACR2

ISBN 0-917298-04-7

Contents

Preface 5

F. Jay Haynes (1853-1921) 7

Small Town Beginnings 19

The Traveling Photographer 49

On the Northern Pacific 77

Recording Life in the West 109

In Yellow Stone Country 139

Haynes' Vision of the Landscape 169

Note on Research Materials 190

Reference List of Illustrations 190

Preface

There was no question in May 1978, when Isabel M. Haynes of Bozeman, Montana, generously donated the magnificent Haynes Photograph Collection to the Montana Historical Society, that we had acquired a great and unique collection — one that featured stunning images taken of the American West during an eighty-year period and documented the dynamic growth of the Northwest. Here, in the 23,500 extant photographs of F. Jay Haynes (1853-1921) and his son Jack Ellis Haynes (1884-1962), is an historical treasury of scenes as remote from one another as Alaska and Minnesota, as different as the winter isolation of Yellowstone geysers and the cosmopolitan bustle of downtown Seattle, as distinct as the Northern Pacific bridging the Missouri River and the ceremonies celebrating the completion of its transcontinental line.

There are images that the Society knew had to be shared with a broad public, and so it is that we have produced this volume, a selection of some of the best photographs taken by F. Jay Haynes, from his earliest days in Minnesota to turn-of-the-century views of Yellowstone National Park. The book is not an attempt to document Haynes' remarkable career as official photographer of the Northern Pacific Railroad and Yellowstone National Park, nor is it meant to highlight any one period of his life. *F. Jay Haynes, Photographer* is a sampler of the rich Haynes Photograph Collection. It is, at the same time, a documentary view of the halcyon years of the development of the Northwest and a selective look at one man's artistic vision of the West.

The book has two parts: an introductory overview of F. Jay Haynes' life and career, with particular emphasis on the development of his photographic businesses, and the presentation of the 160 historical images from the Haynes Photograph Collection. The latter portion is further divided into six general areas that reflect the direction of Haynes' career and the variety of subjects he photographed. Because these photographs are historical artifacts in themselves and because the best possible reproduction was desired, each one has been reproduced faithfully from the highest quality prints made directly from the original wet and dry plate glass negatives. Only in the cases of a few large vertical or permanently masked images have photographs been reduced or cropped.

Each image carries a plate number and an appended identifying caption. The boldface caption entries are photo titles as printed in F. Jay Haynes' several catalogs or as marked on the negatives by the Haynes Studio. A listing of each image reproduced in this book, including those used to illustrate the introductory text, along with relevant technical data can be found in the book's final three pages.

As with any publcation of this size and quality, there are many individuals and organizations to thank. Isbael M. Haynes, widow of Jack Ellis Haynes, protected these materials for many years before donating them to the Montana Historical Society. Without her foresight, exceptional generosity and continued support, this project could not have been conceived. The full and enthusiastic support of the Board of Trustees of the Montana Historical Society was crucial to the project, as was support from the National Historic Publications and Records Commission for preservation of and from the Montana Committee for the Humanities for cataloging of the collection. Montana State University Library's Special Collections graciously made their Haynes materials available for research.

Finally, this book is a product of the combined efforts of the professional staff at the Montana Historical Society. Those who directly contributed to the book are: Robert Clark, Brian Cockhill, Barbara Fifer, Mary Fleenor, William L. Lang, Lory Morrow, Amy Stark, David Walter. We are proud and pleased to present these exceptional photographs by a superb frontier phtoographer to the broadest possible audience.

Robert Archibald
Director
Montana Historical Society

F. Jay Haynes (1853-1921)

NEW PHOTOGRAPH ROOMS

F. Jay Haynes desires to announce that by the first of the coming week his Photograph Rooms, on First Street, will be opened to the public, and those desiring Pictures for the Holliday's should call at once. Carte de vesits, Cabinets, Prominades, 8x10s for Framing, Alba Types or Porcelains, Tin types, etc., etc. Copying in all its branches. Come and see for yourself.

(Moorhead) RED RIVER STAR, December 14, 1876

With this announcement Frank Jay Haynes embarked on a distinguished forty-five-year photographic career that would take him throughout the North American West. Photographing landscapes, special events, frontier towns and people from the Great Lakes to the Pacific Coast, from Manitoba to Alaska, and most notably in Yellowstone National Park, Haynes introduced many inquisitive Americans to the nineteenth-century West. As official photographer for the Northern Pacific Railroad and Yellowstone National Park, he did much to popularize and promote the West. But in September 1876, he was just beginning. The twenty-two-year-old arrived in Moorhead, Minnesota, where the Northern Pacific bridged the Red River, on September 7, 1876 — with but ten cents in his pocket, a "trunk full of Mixture, a stereo box and lenses, and twenty-five dollars worth of chemicals."

In Moorhead, Haynes boarded with his older sister, Ella, and her tinsmith-merchant husband, Gus Henderson. Haynes survived the first months of acclimation to frontier commercial conditions by combining the Hendersons' emotional and financial support with his own aggressive business sense.

> . . . I was bound not to be discouraged, I commenced to make up my chemicals and make some views. I ordered some $60 worth more from Mr. Bode in Milwaukee, Henderson saying "O.K." I then viewed in Moorhead and Fargo. . . . And now here I am, as Nat Kauppen, our *Red River Star* editor says, "Jerking Shadows."

Frank Jay Haynes was born in Saline, Michigan, on October 28, 1853, the third of Levi Hasbrouck and Caroline Oliphant Haynes' six sons. Levi, a merchant and agent for consigned goods, recently had re-located in Saline, about thirty miles southwest of Detroit. The boy worked in his father's store throughout his years of formal education, about which he often noted, "I can see now myself that I quit school too early." By age nineteen he had taken rooms above his father's store and was responsible for its daily operations.

Two years later, in 1874, Haynes added to his responsibilities by taking on a position as a local agent for the New Wilson Sewing Machine Company. In that commissioned capacity, he traveled the countryside while maintaining his father's business in Saline. His other interests, however, proved to be distracting. "October 28, 1873: *My 20th Birthday*. RESOLVED: That I pay all my debts so as to owe none in one year. Also: To *quit* Playing Billiards and Bumming."

The national Panic of 1873 caught Levi Haynes in an overextended financial position, the result of relocating his mercantile in a much larger building in Saline. Soon Levi and Caroline, with the younger children, moved to Detroit, where he gained a position as traveling representative for Perrin's Lubricating Oils. With the demise of his father's mercantile business in 1874, Haynes' experience as a sewing-machine agent offered him alternative employment. In May he agreed to work with Allen H. Risdon, of Ann Arbor, the owner and operator of "Risdon's Western Art Gallery." Haynes became his assistant, at the rate of twenty-five dollars per month. Risdon's itinerant sales wagon for several years had worked the Michigan countryside, offering representations of popular culture to rural inhabitants. The nucleus of the operation was the "chromo wagon," from which Risdon sold chromolithographs, along with sheet music, small plaster busts of noted composers, replacement parts and strings for musical instruments, and wooden, parlor knick-knacks.

With Allen Risdon, Haynes traveled by rail via Chicago and Milwaukee to Whitewater, Wisconsin. At this point the horse-drawn "Western Art Gallery" began its summer tour of the southern Wisconsin farmland, and the Risdon-Haynes routine commenced. While Haynes sold some of the merchandise from a rented building in one town, Risdon drove the country roads to the next major town. Here he engaged in

In a rare picture of the "wet plate" photography process, F. Jay Haynes polishes a glass plate with alcohol and rottenstone. This was the second of five steps that turned a piece of glass into a photographic plate, a process made obsolete around 1880. The picture of Haynes was done about 1875, when he worked for Lockwood's Temple of Photography.

Haynes drove this "view wagon" for Lockwood on summer tours of towns in the Wisconsin countryside. Lettering toward camera reads "Agency for Lockwood's Model Gallery." The side not visible advertises "Landscape Photography by F. J. Haynes."

employment with Graham introduce the former peddler to the mysteries of tintype and stereoscopic photography, but it also combined photography with the sale of views and related items of illustration.

Haynes left Graham's employment in Beaver Dam during the middle of March 1875. He had determined to pursue his interest in photography and, based on his apprenticeship, he sought work with a noted area photographer, "Doctor" William H. Lockwood of Ripon, Wisconsin. Lockwood's "Temple of Photography" produced studio portraits, commercial and residential photos, and landscape views — including the increasingly popular stereoscopic cards. Haynes began work on April 12, 1875, as a general helper, plate preparator, and occasional photo printer, at the contracted wage of twenty-five dollars per month.

He remained with the Lockwoods for almost sixteen months. During this period he developed the skills with tintypes and stereographs that would prepare him for his Moorhead venture. He also became involved in constructing and operating a "view wagon," which he took on summer circuits from Ripon into the countryside. From the horse-drawn view wagon, Haynes took portraits of rural people, group photographs, and outdoor views of their farms. He also operated William Lockwood's excursion boat, "Camera," at nearby Green Lake Resort; the ride included group photos. As Haynes remarked, in the summer of 1876, "I am Pilot, Captain, Conductor, and Artist on the Boat, also . . . throwing out the ropes."

Working for Lockwood changed his personal life, too. Two days after joining the staff at the "Temple of Photography," Haynes met Lily Verna Snyder, the sister of Mrs. Ada Lockwood. Lily, like her sisters Lucy and Loa, periodically worked in the Ripon studio retouching negatives. An obvious affection quickly developed between Haynes and Lily, despite the opposition of both William and Ada Lockwood. And it was not long before friction began between Haynes and his employer. The younger photographer now gave serious thought to striking out on his own. As he wrote to Lily in 1876, "I have come to the conclusion that I can do as well anywheres as I can here, and would not hesitate one moment [to move] if I thought there could be an improvement."

advance promotion for the trailing Haynes and secured another vacant store for their temporary use. Haynes — after selling for a full week in the larger communities, and for only a few days in the smaller towns — packed his cases of merchandise and overtook Risdon by train. Then the sequence began anew.

After several weeks of disappointing sales, the pair separated and Haynes found himself abandoned in the Wisconsin farmland, with little money and no immediate prospects. For two months the thin, mustachioed young man wandered the east-central Wisconsin countryside, practically destitute and relying on the consignments and sales of a bottled furniture remedy, "Haynes' Japanese Polish" — a trunkful of which he fortunately had carried from Michigan. This sobering experience of commercial failure made him determined to secure more stable employment. Finally, at the close of August 1874, Haynes found a job with S. C. Graham, an illustration salesman and photographer with a shop in Beaver Dam, Wisconsin.

For the next seven months, young Haynes worked for the first time with photographic materials. By November of 1874 Graham confidently dispatched the apprentice on a circuit of nearby towns. In this capacity, Haynes shot basic, studio tintype portraits. He also consigned and retailed books of poetry, sheet music, stereoscopic cards and photo views by Midwestern photographers, chromolithographs, picture frames, and photo albums. Not only did this

After much coaxing from his sister, Ella, who had settled in Moorhead, Minnesota, with her husband, Gus Henderson, a hardware-store owner, Haynes decided to accept the Henderson offer to underwrite his move to Moorhead. He was reluctant to leave Lily but his disagreement with Lockwood finally forced the issue in the fall of 1876. After sending Haynes to Oshkosh to work for two weeks, William Lockwood severed Haynes' employment early in September. By September 4, Haynes booked coach passage to Moorhead. He carried with him a determination to prove to the Lockwoods that he could succeed as a commercial photographer, and to show Lily that, financially, he was worthy of her hand.

Fortunately for F. Jay Haynes, the Fargo-Moorhead area needed a skilled photographer. He outfitted a printroom in the Hendersons' home and enjoyed an immediate, if short-lived, rush of orders for portraits, group photos, and commercial exteriors. Haynes knew, however, from his view-wagon experiences, that landscape views would bring additional, long-term income, and he was aware of the regional and national markets for distinctive stereoscopic views.

Haynes turned his camera to the "bonanza farms" in the Red River Valley, large agricultural operations that could cultivate as much as 30,000 acres and seasonally employ hundreds of men. He recognized the novel aspect of such operations at the Dalrymple, at the Grandin, and at the Amenia and Sharon Farms, and he found a ready market for these views. The Northern Pacific Railroad, desirous of promotional photographs of the "bonanza farms," sent Haynes to the Dalrymple Farm in October 1876.

This initial contract with the Northern Pacific proved pivotal to the career of F. Jay Haynes. H. A. Towne, the local superintendent of the Northern Pacific, located in Brainerd, Minnesota, desperately sought a resident photographer who could produce high-quality views along the mainline for documentary and promotional purposes. Pleased with Haynes' work at the Dalrymple Farm, Towne commissioned Haynes, in November 1876, to take stereo views of trackside subjects across the entire division, from Brainerd to the end of the line in Bismarck, Dakota Territory.

Based on Towne's assurance of additional contract work during the 1877 season, Haynes decided to erect a studio in Moorhead, using funds borrowed from Gus Henderson, on land belonging to Gus Henderson. As the construction of his gallery neared completion in early December 1876, Haynes wrote excitedly to Lily:

> The "Shadow Jerking Institution" has assumed its bigness and form and suits me in every respect. By next Monday I will be saying, "Raise your chin," and "Pull down your vest," in my own Gallery.
>
> You see, it is impossible for me to write a letter without speaking of my

Gallery, Views, Prospects, etc. But, Lillie, my mind is all taken up with the "Beautifull Art," and [I] cannot write a letter to anybody without speaking something about Photos.

Haynes occupied his new studio, on First Street in Moorhead, on December 13, 1876. Business built steadily and, through the winter months, he prospered.

Haynes traveled throughout the Moorhead area in 1877 taking stereo views, returning periodically to his studio, where he invested long hours in producing studio portraits and in processing stereo cards. Even as he created an inventory of views for distribution throughout the Midwest, the attraction of the "Yellowstone Country" commenced its pull on him. He wrote to Loa Snyder in May 1877:

> . . . I had a splendid opportunity of visiting the Yellowstone Country this Spring. Col. Moore — who married a cousin of mine at Coldwater, Michigan — is stationed at Fort Buford, and he was anxious I should go with him. But business was such at home that I could not leave.

Haynes' business more and more became his work for the Northern Pacific Railroad. With a permanent railroad pass and payment of $1.50 for each view he produced, it is clear why he exclaimed: ". . . I never saw Business until I came to this Country." Superintendent Towne sent Haynes to various operations served by the line: from the Brainerd railroad yards to activities on the Dalrymple Farm; from the depot at Duluth to natives clustered at Fort Lincoln; from steamboats at the Bismarck levee to hunting parties in N.P. observation cars. And continually Haynes shot supplemental views, which he could market privately.

In September 1877, Haynes exhibited for the first time at the Minnesota State Fair in St. Paul. His stereo views of Dakota subjects caused a genuine stir among fairgoers. The N.P. was pleased. By October Haynes received a new assignment, his first truly "Western" excursion, to the gold-rush camps of the Black Hills.

Commissioned by the Black Hills Stage Company, a subsidiary of the Northern Pacific, Haynes produced views of transportation, commercial, and mining activities in Lead, Central City, Deadwood, and Crook City, Dakota Territory. This five-week trip convinced the photographer that his future could not be separated from the development of the American West. As he noted in a letter to Lily from Crook City:

"Doctor" William H. Lockwood's establishment in Ripon, Wisconsin (above), was the last place where the young Haynes worked before setting out on his own. Haynes' first studio (below), opened in Moorhead, Minnesota, in 1876 — comparatively crude, but a success from its beginning.

. . . The N.P.Rr. Company are commencing construction of their road west of the Missouri [River, at Bismarck]. By next fall they will be in the Yellow Stone Country, and I am in hopes of getting views there. You know, Lillie, the Western country suits me splendidly. I am sorry you have such an awful idea of this country. It is undoubtedly rough, but there is still some fine people here.

His introduction to this slice of Western life occurred in Deadwood, during October of 1877, following a 240-mile stagecoach trip from Bismarck. He was fascinated by the vitality and by the evident recklessness of the booming community, as he wrote to Lily:

. . . Today I believe is Sunday, but from general appearances I don't believe anybody knows it, for the town is livelier today than it has been any day since I arrived. . . . The Town is composed chiefly of Saloons, Gambling Houses, Dance Houses, etc. They have 2 theatres, the "Bella Union" and the "Gem," with lady "beer jerkers," that is, ladies who wait on customers with beer, cigars, and drinks generally. . . . I visited some of the Faro Rooms and saw from 150 to 200 men gambling, and also Keno Rooms which are patronized by a large number. Another place of amusement is the China Pipe Room, run by Chinamen, who have the opium pipe and charge $1.00 for a smoke. The smoker immediately goes into a sort of a swoon and generally stays stupid from 2 to 4 hours.

Much as the Black Hills experience convinced Haynes that western life was personally compatible, it reenforced his belief that a skillful photographer, who aggressively sought contracts and markets, could become a commercial success in the West. And the Deadwood trip convinced Haynes that his photographic future rested with views — commissioned exteriors, landscape compositions, and the novel natural subject. "I have been quite busy since my return," he wrote Lily in November 1877, "making sittings, printing, filling orders, etc. I wish I could make nothing but views, it's much pleasanter, even if it's more work. Everybody wants to see the Black Hills Views; whether they buy any or not, they must look at them."

He began, even at this early juncture, to

experiment with the techniques of view-making. The process captured his imagination and stimulated his creativity. "People generally think that the higher one is, the better the view," he told Lily. "It looks nice from a high point when one has a field glass to enlarge, but when the same view is photographed and condensed, the effect is not as pleasing. . . . There is something that makes my blood run cold when standing where 'the view suits me exactly.'"

For the next several years, F. Jay Haynes continued to develop his skills as a studio-portrait and view photographer, while he solidified his commercial base in the Fargo-Moorhead area. After achieving his goal in the summer of 1877, of earning $1000 above expenses, Haynes married Lily Snyder in Wisconsin in January 1878. The two thereafter operated the Moorhead studio with real diligence, offering photographs in several forms, a full selection of frames and albums, chromolithographs, sheet music, musical instruments — from pianos to trombones to violins — and replacement parts. Simultaneously he continued under contract to the Northern Pacific, documenting the mainline's extension west of Bismarck as well as numerous trackside subjects.

The Haynes Studio, with a considerable inventory of stereo views that were wholesaled to dealers in the Midwest and East, published its first catalog of stereo views in 1879, available directly to the general public; it featured bonanza-farm subjects. By 1881 the Studio's inventory included many Northern Pacific, Black Hills, Missouri River steamboat, and Badlands view sets.

In October 1878 Lily and F. Jay Haynes became parents of a girl they named Bessie Loa. The press of business, however, returned Lily to the studio to retouch negatives and to oversee gallery operations while F. Jay traveled. And the business grew. In May 1879, Haynes moved to a new, larger studio in Fargo, from which he would operate for the next ten years.

His increased business required assistants, to perform plate-preparation and printing duties, and to assemble orders. Although scores of employees worked for Haynes during his career, the most constant was James Paris, whom he had met when both worked for Lockwood in Wisconsin. During the summer of 1880, Paris joined the staff at the Fargo studio; he remained with the Haynes operation until 1905. Haynes entrusted the most important assignments to Paris, including negative retouching, high-quality printing for special albums, photo tinting, and general assistance on commissioned trips. In 1888 the Haynes Gallery employed thirteen people; in the late 1890s, the seasonal photographic staff exceeded

Lily Snyder Haynes and F. Jay Haynes pose, about the time of their marriage in January 1878.

twenty.

The season of 1881 proved particularly significant for F. Jay Haynes' evolving photographic career. During July and August, he worked an extended commission for the Northern Pacific Railroad, for the St. Paul, Minneapolis, and Manitoba Railway, and for the Canadian Pacific Railway, which sent him to Canada, designated him the "authorized photographer" for each railroad, and specified his usual terms: one dozen prints to the respective company from each negative, at cost; retention of the negatives by Haynes; permission for Haynes to market these and any other views obtained on the trips. The rail lines supplied transportation, room, and board.

The Canadian expedition took Haynes from Fargo to Winnipeg, Manitoba, from where he operated for seven weeks, included horse, canoe, buggy, and foot travel, into several truly remote areas of southern Canada. The Canadian excursion convinced Haynes that he could rely on his photographic business for financial security.

Once he returned to Fargo, Haynes extricated himself from the musical-instrument trade and embarked on another commission for the Northern Pacific Railroad. This one would change his life. The N.P.'s passenger agent in St. Paul, Charles S. Fee — with whom the photographer had developed a mutually beneficial contract relationship — arranged a view-taking expedition for him to Yellowstone National Park. In late August 1881, Haynes left the end-of-track at Glendive, Montana Territory, and traveled to Bozeman by stage; from Bozeman the party used a horse and wagon, remaining in the Park most of September.

The splendor and novelty of the Park's natural features enthralled him. He realized immediately that, to a photographer of views, Yellowstone truly offered the possibilities of a "Wonderland."

That he perceived the commercial possibilities of Yellowstone National Park is evident from his immediate attempt to obtain a franchise from the Department of the Interior to establish a photographic operation in the Upper Geyser Basin. Although he did not obtain the concession until 1884, Haynes returned to Yellowstone in 1882 and every year thereafter for the remainder of his life — to photograph, process, and sell views of the "Wonderland." Still, Haynes recognized that the foundation of his photographic operation rested with the Fargo studio work and with Passenger Agent Charles S. Fee's series of contracts for the Northern Pacific Railroad.

In 1879 the N.P. had commenced construction of

1528. HELL'S HALF ACRE, FIRE HOLE RIVER.

Haynes (on footbridge) and an assistant examine the overflow of Excelsior Geyser into the Firehole River, Yellowstone National Park, 1883. He titled the above scene "Hell's Half Acre."

the mainline east from Tacoma, Washington Territory, and west from Bismarck — where crews seasonally alternated using an ice bridge and a transfer steamboat to cross the Missouri River to Mandan. For the next four years, grading and tracking proceeded from each end, until the lines officially joined at Gold Creek, Montana Territory, on September 8, 1883. During this period, Fee contracted Haynes to document track construction and to produce views of trackside towns, businesses, and natural features to illustrate N.P. promotional literature. Haynes retained the negatives and reserved the prerogative of taking additional views to expand his personal inventory.

During the 1882 season, Haynes traveled the Northern Pacific right-of-way from Bismarck to Missoula, Montana Territory, and then to Yellowstone for two months because the railroad wanted to promote tourist traffic along its lines to the Park. On this tour Haynes first experimented with dry plates in the Park. Meanwhile, Lily managed the expanding business of the Fargo studio.

While working to establish himself as the preeminent photographer of Yellowstone National Park features during the 1883 season, he also drew Northern Pacific assignments that carried him from St. Paul to Portland, Oregon, and from Fargo to Tacoma. Back in Yellowstone in July 1883, Haynes was appointed "official photographer" for President Chester A. Arthur's excursion party through

Haynes posed formally for another, unidentified, photographer in this 1882 portrait.

Haynes photographed his newly erected Mammoth Hot Springs headquarters in Yellowstone about 1884. Plate 132 shows its changed appearance fourteen years later.

Yellowstone. It was a big party "of 47 pack mules each, 54 Cavalry men, 2 scouts, 6 Indian guides, servants and cooks, packers, etc.," Haynes wrote to Lily. "I have a tent to myself and a man to put it up and wait on me whenever I want anything."

He left the Presidential party early in September and exited the Park via the new Northern Pacific branch-line terminal at Cinnabar, Montana. He immediately joined the "Villard Excursion Train" in St. Paul, beginning a journey of six weeks that would lead him as far west as Seattle, Washington Territory.

In September 1882, the gap between the two portions of the Northern Pacific Railroad's mainline stretched almost five hundred miles, from Park City west to Thompson Falls, Montana Territory. Through a massive construction effort — elements of which Haynes photographed — the two sections joined at Gold Creek on August 23, 1883. To celebrate the completion of the first northern transcontinental mainline, and the Yellowstone branch-line to Cinnabar, Northern Pacific President Henry Villard organized a 30-day excursion, at the railroad's expense, through the Northwest for more than 300 select guests.

The highlight of the $200,000 tour occurred when the 44-car "Gold Spike Special" reached Gold Creek. Here, on September 8, a crowd of approximately 4,000 people witnessed the symbolic driving of the final spike by dignitaries including Ex-President Ulysses S. Grant. Haynes' photographs of this celebration are among his most widely distributed. The photographer then accompanied one of the "Excursion Train's" sections on a tour of the Pacific Northwest, returning to Fargo by the middle of October.

The Northern Pacific Railroad appreciated Haynes' diligent photographic work in its behalf. In May 1883, the Yellowstone Park Improvement Company, an organization closely aligned with the N.P., designated F. Jay Haynes the "Official Photographer for the Y.P.I.C., also Superintendent of the Art Department, with Headquarters at the Mammoth Hot Springs, Wyoming." Prior to the "Gold Spike" festivities in September 1883, the Northern Pacific also designated Frank its "Official Photographer," a title he would retain until 1905.

In July 1882, Haynes had returned to Yellowstone, armed with a camera capable of producing larger negatives. At the urging of N.P. Passenger Agent Charles Fee, he sought additional Park views that the Northern Pacific could employ in advertising its pending rail access to the Yellowstone wonders. On this trip he applied his annual N.P. pass to the end-of-track construction near Billings, Montana Territory, and there obtained a horse and wagon, a packer, and a guide to accompany him. Haynes remained in the Park into September on this outing, returning to Fargo more convinced than ever that his future rested among the geysers, waterfalls, lakes, and mountain splendor. When the Yellowstone Park Improvement Company named him "Official Photographer" (1883), it only recognized what he already had determined as his role in the development of Yellowstone.

Following his first trip to the "Wonderland" in 1881, Haynes had begun seeking a Department of the Interior franchise to operate a photographic studio within the reserve. Because Yellowstone had been created the nation's first national park a mere nine years earlier, the Washington, D.C., office remained uncertain about the conferring of such leases, concessions, or franchises. After submitting additional applications in 1882, 1883, and early 1884, F. Jay Haynes finally received the first concessionaire lease granted for Yellowstone National Park. As stipulated by the Acting Secretary of the Interior, on March 20, 1884, Haynes was given a lease for eight acres in the Upper Geyser Basin (Old Faithful area), "with the privilege of erecting thereon a building or buildings, as may be required for the purpose of preparing photographic views of the objects of interest in the park, for sale to tourists."

At the close of the 1884 season, the Department agreed to modify the lease, permitting a division of the eight acres into two four-acre parcels. The first of these pieces retained part of the original Upper Geyser Basin site and the second established a base in the

Mammoth Hot Springs locale. By 1885, Haynes operated two photo outlets, serving visitors and providing bases for his continued photographic exploration of the Park, with his headquarters at Mammoth Hot Springs — within easy access of the North Entrance and the Northern Pacific railhead at Cinnabar. At Mammoth he erected a prefabricated, frame studio/residence and surrounded it with distinctive elkhorn fencing. This gallery and the Haynes Log Cabin Studio — built in 1897 close to the Old Faithful Inn — remained the center of his photographic network in Yellowstone for thirty years.

During the mid-1880s, the Northern Pacific Railroad conducted an extensive publicity campaign, seeking passenger traffic to Yellowstone Park and to the West Coast, settlers for its land-grant properties, and always the increase of trackside commerce, which would translate into freight profits. Haynes produced views to illustrate the N.P.'s booster publications, which necessitated expanding his studio staff at Fargo. Simultaneously he established branch operations in Yellowstone National Park and continued the national distribution of his "Wonderland" and regional stereoscopic views.

The Haynes Palace Studio Car, during its twenty years of operation (1885-1905), became a welcomed institution in towns and cities along the Northern Pacific's various lines. His idea for the car derived from his earlier experiences with Risdon's "Chromo Wagon" and Lockwood's "View Wagon"; he simply meshed that concept with the available N.P. equipment that was familiar to him.

Haynes designed the original Palace Studio Car during the winter of 1884-1885. In the spring of 1885, F. Jay and James Paris traveled to the N.P.'s Brainerd yards, where they supervised the remodeling of a Pullman car, christened the "Yellowstone." The contract between Haynes and the Northern Pacific for the car specified payments totaling six thousand dollars over a two-year period. By the end of September 1885, the car began its maiden tour.

The Palace Car featured a heated reception room for waiting customers, a studio room, a dark room with appropriate processing and storage facilities, and living quarters for two. The studio, or "operating room," contained the cameras, useful props, and a selection of painted, canvas backdrops — depicting a sunlit garden, a scholarly library, a cozy sitting room, or some other scene — to fit the customer's desires. During the 1880s, Haynes often operated the car himself during the winter months, detailing it to two of his assistants in the summer, so he could pursue his Yellowstone Park enterprises. Brother Fred Haynes, James Paris, and Hiram H. Wilcox most frequently worked the tours in the 1890s, although F. Jay arranged the itinerary and carefully supervised the operation. For thousands of people from Duluth, Minnesota, to Olympia, Washington, who would never visit Yellowstone National Park, Haynes was famous for his Palace Studio Car. Its location on a sidetrack

Samples of Haynes' art filled the waiting room of his Palace Studio Car when he photographed it on November 30, 1886.

This 1901 view of the Palace Studio Car shows the elaborately lettered advertisements that drew customers at every stop: Artistic Photography in all its Branches; F. Jay Haynes. Official Photographer. Northern Pacific; Northern Pacific and National Park Views.

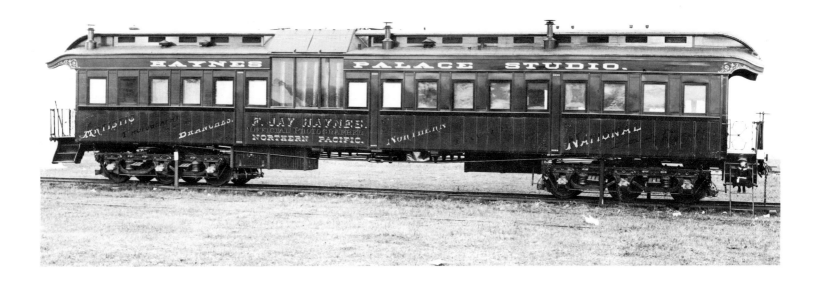

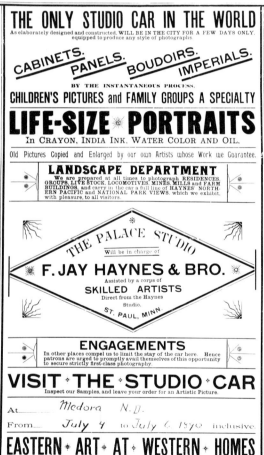
near any town's depot produced great excitement among the citizens.

The Palace Studio Car permitted Haynes, or one of his reliable assistants, to obtain additional trackside stereos to enlarge his "Northern Pacific Views" offerings. For instance, in July 1886, Haynes left Yellowstone for a month to produce hundreds of negatives of Northern Pacific subjects in Montana and along the Columbia River. In August of both 1887 and 1888, he made similar tours, running from Wyoming through Montana, Idaho, Washington, and Oregon. After 1889, though, Haynes managed to coordinate most of his N.P. contract work with the annual, sweeping tours of the Palace Car.

One of his last contracted trips arranged by the Northern Pacific Railroad involved a steamship cruise in 1891 from Tacoma to Wrangell, Juneau, Sitka, and Glacier Bay, Alaska, and return. He undertook this commission for the Puget Sound and Alaska Steamship Company, which the N.P. would purchase in 1892. Haynes and Paris traveled on three ships — the *Queen,* the *Mexico,* and the *City of Topeka* — and returned with a number of dramatic negatives for the companies.

Haynes continued to produce commissioned trackside photographs for the Northern Pacific Railroad through 1904, when he retired the Haynes Palace Studio Car from operation. By that time, however, the direction of his photographic business had shifted and coalesced somewhat. He gradually relied more upon qualified assistants to manage the Fargo studio work and the Palace Car tours — liberating himself for seasonal activities in Yellowstone National Park. He further consolidated his operations in 1889 by moving his studio from Fargo to St. Paul, where he established the new gallery at the corner of Jackson and Sixth Streets. Charles S. Fee had suggested this transfer, for the mutual benefit of the railroad and its "Official Photographer." Then, during the winters, Haynes traveled through the Midwest and the East to solicit dealers for his view selections, to consult with photographic houses concerning new equipment, and to exhibit his photos — as he did at the Chicago World's Fair (World's Columbian Exhibition) in 1893.

F. Jay Haynes, by the end of the 1890s, reorganized his several photo enterprises in two locations, Yellowstone National Park during the tourist season and St. Paul during the remainder of the year. His attention riveted on Yellowstone, where he applied his accumulated business knowledge as well as his creative photographic expertise. As he gradually

expanded his retail facilities in the Park, he continued to build the most extensive inventory of photographs of Yellowstone subjects ever assembled. Because of the international advertising produced by the passenger departments of the Northern Pacific and the Union Pacific Railroads, Haynes photographs frequently determined the tourist's first impression of the Park. After visiting Yellowstone, that tourist often exited in possession of several Haynes views to commemorate the trip.

Haynes used his camera to see and capture Yellowstone as no one else could. In this pursuit he participated in two winter trips into Yellowstone, the first in 1887 and another in 1894. In the former instance, the *New York World* commissioned him to accompany the noted Arctic explorer Lieutenant Frederick Schwatka on the maiden winter expedition into the Park. Haynes joined the group at Cinnabar early in January 1887. The eight-man expedition struggled for six days to ski the twenty-five miles into the primitive hotel at the Norris Geyser Basin. By this time, snow conditions had forced the party to abandon its toboggans, bearpaw snowshoes, and other superfluous equipment, and the group had suffered overnight temperatures as low as thirty-seven degrees below zero.

Just south of the Norris Hotel, Lieutenant Schwatka developed hemorrhaging lungs, and his participation in the expedition ceased. But F. Jay Haynes was determined to obtain winter photos. He persuaded two members of the original party, Charles A. Stoddard and David Stratton, to join him; he also contacted resident Yellowstone scout Edward Wilson to meet them at the Upper Geyser Basin and to serve as guide. The "Hard Winter of 1886-1887" became notorious for the cattle devastation it precipitated on the Montana-Wyoming open ranges — yet in this weather the "Haynes Winter Expedition" proceeded.

Despite a five-day storm in the Upper Geyser Basin, Haynes managed some dramatic geyser photos in the Old Faithful area. The men then retraced their ski trail to the Norris Hotel and worked their way east, toward the Canyon Hotel, to capture shots of the ice-encrusted Great Falls of the Yellowstone. From the Canyon, Wilson led the party northeast, over the Washburn Range to "Yancey's Pleasant Valley Hotel" near Tower Fall, and thence west over the Cooke City wagon track to Mammoth. On the initial leg of this return journey, the expedition encountered its most severe weather: the minimally supplied skiers became marooned on the slopes of Mount Washburn for the duration of a howling, two-day blizzard. They barely survived the ordeal. Haynes subsequently billed his "Yellowstone Park in Winter" photograph series, which proved an immediate financial success: "Views Gained at the Greatest Personal Peril to the Photographer."

Seven years later, Haynes received the opportunity to increase his inventory of winter photographs of Yellowstone. Under the auspices of the conservationistic weekly *Forest and Stream,* Editor George Bird Grinnell paired Haynes with famed writer Emerson Hough for a reconnaissance of the wildlife wintering in the Park. The excursion consumed much of the month of March 1894, but the cloud cover never cleared sufficiently for Haynes to obtain really remarkable winter photos.

By 1908, F. Jay Haynes had realigned his railroad associations. The Haynes Palace Studio Car ceased operating on the Northern Pacific lines after the 1904 tour and, thereafter, N.P. officials contracted other photographers for trackside views. Also in 1904, Haynes' friend Charles S. Fee left the Northern Pacific to assume the position of passenger traffic manager with the Southern Pacific, a Union Pacific affiliate with offices in San Francisco.

By 1916, Haynes had disengaged himself from the Northern Pacific and acquired a better concession agreement with the new National Park Service. 1916 also proved significant to Haynes' activities in Yellowstone, because at this time he transferred his complete photographic interests to his son, Jack Ellis Haynes. Subsequently, Haynes' annual trips to the park cast him in the role of "Yellowstone Patriarch." Through his last stay in Yellowstone, during the 1920 season, Haynes became a familiar sight traveling the Park's roads. Some other Yellowstone old-timer or dignitary often accompanied him on these tours among the "Wonderland's" unusual features — all of which he had photographed for decades. Finally Haynes could abandon his lifelong, hectic work schedule and could enjoy the amenities of a career that had begun in the fledgling settlement of Moorhead, Minnesota, more than forty years earlier.

Haynes' health had begun to deteriorate prior to his transfer of the family enterprises to his son. Still he arrived in his cherished Yellowstone Park each summer and returned to the Haynes home in St. Paul each autumn. At his home, on March 10, 1921, F. Jay Haynes succumbed to heart complications at the age of sixty-seven, while surrounded by his immediate family. The Director of the National Park Service responded at once with a directive for all flags in Yellowstone Park to fly at half-mast for a period of one

Special Collections, Montana State Univ., Bozeman

F. JAY HAYNES'
National Park Studio.

In Front of the National Hotel,

MAMMOTH HOT SPRINGS.

Most Complete Line of Park Views Published, from Stereoscopic to Twenty by Twenty-four. Also NATIONAL PARK SOUVENIR ALBUMS.

GROUPS OF PRIVATE PARTIES A SPECIALTY.

Headquarters for Tourists, Artists and Amateur Photographers.

The Haynes sales counter in Yellowstone Park's National Hotel, about 1892, displayed the many sizes and types of park views offered to tourists, as enumerated in the advertisement above.

month.

Park officials and personal friends then sought a more permanent commemoration of his contributions to the "Wonderland." Yellowstone Superintendent Horace M. Albright (1919-1929) proposed the naming of the West Entrance for Haynes. Proponents abandoned this proposal, however, in favor of naming an 8,235-foot mountain peak in the Madison River Canyon for him. Thus "Mount Haynes" rises just inside the boundary of Yellowstone Park to overlook the West Entrance, a perpetual reminder of the photographer-concessionaire's sympathetic involvement in the Park's publicity and development.

Yet Haynes experienced a career much more diverse then the title "Official Photographer of Yellowstone National Park" indicates. From his adolescent mercantile experiences in Michigan to his early photographic training with Graham and Lockwood in Wisconsin, this complex young man demonstrated a remarkable affinity for combining

In their skylighted studio, retouching artists work on portraits and Yellowstone National Park views at the Haynes Gallery, St. Paul, Minnesota, in 1893. Left to right, they are identified as: Frisbie, James Paris, Frank E. Scott, unidentified woman.

technical skills, creativity and marketing sense. His Fargo-Moorhead phase (1876-1889) provided the opportunity for him to expand and hone those skills, to build a photographic reputation as a fine photographer deserving the distinction "Official Photographer of the Northern Pacific Railroad." Between St. Paul and Tacoma, and from the Upper Geyser Basin to Alaska, Haynes assembled a sensitive record of the landscape through which he moved.

More than a middle-level Gilded Age capitalist, blessed with a marketable skill and sound business sense, more than a timely chronicler of the American Northwest, Frank Jay Haynes brought great sensitivity to each of his photographic views. The remaining collection of his prints is a superb historical record of the development of the Northwest and an impressive example of a fine photographer's skill and creativity. His photographs — artistically, technically, and historically — are his enduring legacies.

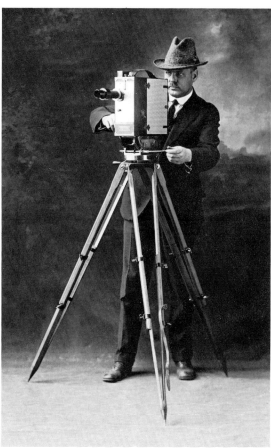

Jack Ellis Haynes (above, posed with a movie camera in 1918) took over his father's Yellowstone Park businesses in 1916. Jack was the photographer for the group portrait at left, taken on December 30, 1913 in the Haynes' St. Paul home. F. Jay Haynes is seated at center, his wife Lily and her sister Loa Jackson to the viewer's right. Standing are, left to right, son George Haynes, and family friends Ralph and Ruth Ely.

Small Town Beginnings

F. Jay Haynes first arrived in Moorhead, Minnesota, on September 7, 1876. The embryonic Red River Valley settlements of Fargo and Moorhead and the frontier locale offered various opportunities to an astute businessman. And Haynes immediately began to seize those opportunities. For the next several years, as a small-town photographer, Haynes laid the foundation for his later photographic success.

Until 1879 the Northern Pacific Railroad reached only as far west as the Bismarck levee, where it connected with the Missouri River steamboat network. Settlement and commercial development along the mainline both depended upon, and were partially instigated by, the Northern Pacific. Haynes received his first N.P. contract to document this growth a mere two months after his arrival. His stereoscopic camera revealed fledgling communities so recently constructed that while fences delineated property lines, the structures lacked shade trees. Haynes also recorded commercial establishments that offered the settler/investor some of the amenities as well as the necessities of eastern life. More than the stores, however, the newspaper office and the train depot were the viable links between the Red River Valley and an industrializing America to the east. In this setting Haynes established his studios, to serve the communities' photographic needs. Steady studio work would remain the commercial basis of the Haynes operation in the West.

Still, Haynes' passion was the exterior view, not the studio portrait. Those early Northern Pacific commissions took him into the Dakota-Minnesota countryside to depict its opportunities and successes. Here he proved his value to the N.P. as a contract photographer, while he assembled saleable view sets of area subjects. The expansion of Red River Valley "bonanza farms" particularly offered photographic possibilities because the farms employed fleets of modern machinery and large crews of men on large acreages. This agricultural phenomenon drew even President Rutherford B. Hayes to the Valley in 1878.

In the late 1870s and early 1880s, Haynes began to capture the subjects that would make him successful as a commercial photographer in the West. He not only recorded Red River Valley farms and towns, but he also recognized the photographic possibilities of such natural curiosities as the spring break-up and the flood. He documented the importance of transportation systems to the West — whether they involved the local grain barge, the Missouri River steamboat, or the Northern Pacific mainline — systems the West depended upon for its settlement, commercial progress, and social evolution. Finally, he discovered the potential for western tourist travel, first by wealthy easterners and then by an emerging American middle class.

F. Jay Haynes developed his photographic skills as a small-town photographer. Unlike contemporary eastern photographers who toured the West, Haynes lived there and learned there.

PLATE 1. **Group at N.P. depot, Bismarck, D.T.** Northern Pacific Railroad depot, June 1877.

PLATE 2. **"Times Office."** Fargo, Dakota Territory, *Times* building, fall 1876.

PLATE 3. **Scholars of Union School.** Fargo, Dakota Territory, 1878.

PLATE 4. **Southwest from Headquarters Hotel, Fargo.** Dakota Territory, October
1876.

24

PLATE 5. J. A. Johnson & Co.'s steam thresher outfit. Headquarters Hotel in background,
Fargo, Dakota Territory, probably 1881.

PLATE 6. **Henderson & Erickson's Block.** Main Street, Moorhead, Minnesota, fall 1876.

PLATE 7. Dining room of G. S. Barnes residence, Fargo, Dakota Territory, 1883.

PLATE 8. **Interior E. A. Grant's Store.** Dry goods store, Fargo, Dakota Territory, fall 1876.

PLATE 9. Bessie Loa Haynes. Studio portrait, with painted background and artificial grass, of the photographer's daughter, Fargo, Dakota Territory, April 1, 1883.

PLATE 10. Lily Snyder Haynes, the photographer's wife, at her writing desk, Fargo, Dakota Territory, circa 1880.

PLATE 11. **Plow Teams, The Spiritwood Farms.** Foremen, on horseback, with single-bladed plows, eighty-three miles west of Fargo along the Northern Pacific line, Dakota Territory, 1880.

315. Breaking.

PLATE 12. **Prairie Breaking (16 teams).** The Dalrymple Farm, twenty miles west of Fargo in the Red River Valley, situated along the Northern Pacific line, 1878.

PLATE 13. **Harvesting with 10 Self-Binders.** Williams wheat farm, thirteen miles west of Fargo in the Red River Valley, Dakota Territory, 1878.

PLATE 14. **Threshing in Red River Valley.** Steam thresher near Glyndon, Minnesota, fall 1878.

PLATE 15. Farm hands at the Barnes & Co. Farm, Glyndon, Minnesota, summer 1879.

35

PLATE 16. **Presidential Excursion Party at Farm.** President Rutherford B. Hayes with a decorated six-car Northern Pacific excursion train, at Dalrymple Farm twenty miles west of Fargo, Dakota Territory, September 6, 1878.

PLATE 17. **Flat Boat Building, Red River.** Boats under construction near Moorhead, Minnesota, fall 1876.

PLATE 18. Union grain elevator and loading dock, along Red River, Fargo, Dakota Territory, probably 1881.

PLATE 19. Steamer *Selkirk,* Moorhead, Minnesota levee. Red River, spring 1877.

PLATE 20. **Bismarck Levee.** Missouri River steamers *Nellie Peck* and *Far West*, June 1877.

PLATE 21. Red River flood, Fargo, Dakota Territory, April 1881.

PLATE 22. Missouri River flood, ice breakup. Mandan, Dakota Territory, spring 1881.

PLATE 23. **City of Worcester at Crystal Springs.** A hunting party with their Northern Pacific Railroad car, Dakota Territory, fall 1878.

PLATE 24. **Interiors of City of Worcester.** Northern Pacific railroad car interior, 1878.

PLATE 25. **Indian Village North of City.** Chippewa Indians at Leech Lake Agency along
the Mississippi River above Brainerd, Minnesota, spring 1877.

PLATE 26. **Medicine Man, Yellow Dog, and Squaws.** Studio portrait with painted background. Left to right: Big Medicine Man, his wife (unidentified), Yellow Dog, his wife seated (unidentified), 1883.

1494 BIG MEDICINE MAN.

PLATE 27: **Big Medicine Man.** Crow Indian, 1883.

PLATE 28. **Yellow Dog.** Crow Indian, 1883.

The Traveling Photographer

F. Jay Haynes is distinguished from many of his contemporaries by his willingness, even impatience, to travel extensively in search of photo views. More than most, he received the opportunity to travel extensively. In 1876, Haynes fulfilled his first commission for the Northern Pacific Railroad Company. For the N.P., and himself over the next thirty years, he crisscrossed the West — from Duluth to Tacoma, from Fort Washakie to Juneau, from Rat Portage to the Great Falls of the Missouri, and from any point to Yellowstone National Park.

By 1879, when the Northern Pacific began its push to close the first northern mainline, Haynes already was the company's authorized photographer. He thereafter documented developments in the West, while providing appropriate photos for the N.P.'s widely disseminated promotional literature.

The Northern Pacific distributed literature with two purposes: to assure prospective settlers that the West was safe and "modern," and to entice prospective investors to locate in the West. Haynes' commissioned photographs reflected these aims. In 1877, for example, he endured an excruciating stagecoach journey from Bismarck to Deadwood, for the Black Hills Stage Company (a subsidiary of the N.P.), to obtain views showing the "stability" of the boom camps and indicating the opportunities available to adventurers — who could reach the location via the Black Hills Stage. The Northern Pacific also wished to quiet fears of the West's inherent danger, and to convince the immigrant-investor not to fear the loss of social and cultural amenities there. Haynes' 1880 steamboat journey on the upper Missouri provided pictures of the regular boat traffic to Fort Benton (head of navigation) and the business community this traffic was creating. He also took scenic views, for his own use, along the water route and beyond the head of navigation, traveling overland to the Great Falls.

A secondary, but lucrative, source of income for the Northern Pacific and its transportation associates involved the growing tourist trade. Haynes sought views of the unusual natural feature or of the geological curiosity that would draw summer visitors west over the N.P.'s lines. By 1885 a distinct American group had emerged: tourists attracted to the West's novelties by prosaic descriptions and stereoscopic photographs. These people seasonally came west wishing to be, literally, *"sight seers."* F. Jay Haynes was prepared. In 1881 he began over two decades of photographing the West's greatest concentration of natural curiosities — the geysers, waterfalls, mountains, hot springs, terraces, lakes, canyons, and mud pools of Yellowstone National Park.

Most often Haynes traveled the West with little assistance, perhaps a single helper and a wagon man. His photographic travels were complicated by the heavy, bulky equipment, by the fragility of glass plates, and by the instability of necessary chemicals. For more than twenty years, he left his gallery each spring, to produce commissioned work throughout the West. He documented transportation construction, and encouraged capital investment and settlement in the region. Most importantly, Haynes' many travels presented the potential American tourist with visions of the wondrous West, visions that demonstrated his photographic skill and made his reputation.

PLATE 29. Wall Street, Deadwood, Black Hills, Dakota Territory, fall 1877.

PLATE 30. **Black Tail Gulch.** Gayville, Black Hills, Dakota Territory, 1877.

PLATE 31. **Signal Hill, Central City.** Dakota Territory, 1877.

569 "OUR ARTIST." MISSOURI RIVER FALLS.

PLATE 32. **Our Artist at the Falls.** F. Jay Haynes with stereoscopic camera at the Great
Falls of the Missouri River, Montana Territory, summer 1880.

PLATE 33. **Landing, Cow Island.** Camp at Cow Island on the Missouri River, Montana
Territory, summer 1880.

579. FORT BENTON, M. T., FROM THE BLUFFS.

PLATE 34. **Fort Benton, from Bluffs.** Fort Benton, Montana Territory, summer 1880.

PLATE 35. **First View of the Bad Lands.** Cedar Canyon in the Badlands of Dakota Territory, spring 1880.

PLATE 36. **"Wooding Up" in the Mountains.** The *Helena* of the "Block P" line, merchant
T. C. Power's Fort Benton Transportation Company, on the Missouri River, summer
1880.

PLATE 37. Mission school at Devils Lake Indian Agency, Fort Totten, Dakota Territory, 1881.

PLATE 38. **Gattling Gun Battery, Fort Totten.** Dakota Territory, 1881.

821. STEAM SHOVER AND SAND PIT.

PLATE 39. **Steam Shovel and Sand Pit.** Steam-powered shovel and construction of
Canadian Pacific Railroad, summer 1881.

796. HUDSON BAY Co.'s POST—RAT PORTAGE.

PLATE 40. **Hudson Bay Co.'s Post, Rat Portage.** Hudson's Bay post, summer 1881.

809. LUMBER YARD—KEEWATIN MILLS.

PLATE 41. **Lumber Yard, Keewatin Mills.** Drying yard for lumber, Ontario, Canada, summer 1881.

807. LOG BOOM—KEEWATIN MILLS.

PLATE 42. **Log Boom, Keewatin Mills.** On the Winnipeg River, Ontario, Canada, summer
1881.

1099. LOWER CANYON OF THE YELLOWSTONE.

PLATE 43. **Lower Canyon of the Yellowstone.** Haynes' wagon on his first trip to
Yellowstone National Park, 1881.

PLATE 44. **The Grand Canyon of the Yellowstone.** The Grand Canyon as seen from
     Inspiration Point, Yellowstone National Park, fall 1881.

PLATE 45. **Lone Star Geyser Cone.** Yellowstone National Park, 1882.

PLATE 46. **A Geyser Immediately After Eruption.** Splendid Geyser crater in Upper Geyser Basin, Yellowstone National Park, 1881.

PLATE 47. **Presidential Party at Upper Geyser Basin.** President Chester A. Arthur's tour of Yellowstone National Park, August 1883. Identified as, standing: Michael V. Sheridan, Anson Stager, W. P. Clark, Dan G. Rollins, James F. Gregory; seated: John S. Crosby, Philip H. Sheridan, President Arthur, Robert T. Lincoln, George G. Vest.

PLATE 48. **Arrapahoe Indian Chiefs, Fort Washakie.** Arapahoe and Shoshone Indians assembled to meet President Arthur's party. Identified as, back row: Cammache, Ute Bob, Wallowing Bull, Ground Bear, Sage, Black Coal; front row, Nam-ma-gan-na-dza, unidentified, Ah-quita's son, Jim Washakie, Nacoita, George Washakie. Fort Washakie, W. T., August 1883.

PLATE 49. **Crevasse in Muir Glacier.** Surface of the Muir Glacier, Alaska, 1891.

PLATE 50. **Str. "Queen" Approaching Muir Glacier.** The steamship *Queen* in Glacier
Bay near Muir Glacier, Alaska, 1891.

PLATE 51. **The Whale, Fort Wrangel.** Totem at Fort Wrangell, Alaska, 1891.

PLATE 52. **Juneau, Alaska.** Harbor and town of Juneau at foot of Mount Roberts, Alaska, 1891.

PLATE 53. W. S. Webb excursion camp on North Fork (Buffalo Fork) in the Teton Range, Wyoming, September 1896.

PLATE 54. W. S. Webb and guide Baptiste on W. S. Webb excursion, Wyoming, September 1896.

On the Northern Pacific

The Northern Pacific Railroad Company figured prominently in the course and content of F. Jay Haynes' photographic career. The competency he displayed in his first Northern Pacific assignment in 1876 led to a series of N.P.-commissioned travels within Canada, to Alaska, and then throughout the American West. Between 1885 and 1905, Haynes regularly set his Palace Studio Car rolling on main and branch line rails in pursuit of N.P. subjects.

In 1876 the Northern Pacific had just suffered bankruptcy and reorganization. Its mainline lay in two sections, an eastern portion running from Duluth to Bismarck, and a western segment stretching between the Columbia River and Tacoma. Two years later the railroad began a five-year construction campaign to close the gap between the two sections.

Haynes' initial contracts with the Northern Pacific required him to produce views of the company's facilities and equipment for its reference files. So, when crews pushed west from Fargo in 1879, Haynes accompanied them to document surveying, grading, and track-laying techniques. He paid special attention to the erection of the Missouri River Bridge between Bismarck and Mandan, because it symbolized the thrust of the railroad across the plains, up the Yellowstone River Valley, and into the Rocky Mountains. In 1882 he also began to record the Pacific Division's progress eastward. Because of the importance of minimal grade to railroad construction Haynes' subjects often included such grade-modifiers as bridges, trestles, cuts and fills, and tunnels.

Northern Pacific President Henry Villard marked the completion of the mainline with an extensive excursion train tour for scores of dignitaries. Elaborate ceremonies at Gold Creek, Montana Territory, on September 8, 1883, highlighted Villard's cross-country tour on the new transcontinental. Thereafter Haynes traveled the entire N.P. network to record track clearings and modifications, as well as the construction of branch lines. And always he supplied the N.P. office in St. Paul with documentary photos of engines, depots, and other trackside facilities and equipment.

As the Northern Pacific developed its operations in the upper Great Plains and in the Northwest, Haynes' role expanded as supplier of informational and promotional photographs for the railroad's publications and exhibitions aimed at both tourists and emigrants. Haynes remained the railroad's "Official Photographer" from 1876 until 1905. During those three decades, he compiled a significant photographic record of the N.P.'s growth, honed his skills as a landscape photographer, and introduced thousands to the art of photography through his Palace Studio Car.

PLATE 55. **Loading N.P. Transfer, Bismarck.** Northern Pacific train being loaded onto
    ferry for Missouri River crossing, spring 1880.

PLATE 56. **Up the Missouri from Levee.** Northern Pacific railroad terminus at Bismarck,
Dakota Territory, fall 1876.

PLATE 57. Construction of the Northern Pacific Railroad bridge over the Missouri River at
Bismarck, Dakota Territory, 1881.

PLATE 58. **Testing the Bismarck Bridge.** Eight Northern Pacific locomotives on one
span of the bridge over the Missouri at Bismarck, October 21, 1882.

PLATE 59. **East Entrance to Mullen Tunnel.** The 3,800-foot Mullan Tunnel, cut through
rock, took from January 1882 to November 22, 1883, to build. Montana Territory,
1883.

PLATE 60. **Big Cut and Sweet Briar Valley.** Workmen with hand tools load dirt from railroad cut onto horse-drawn wagons, Dakota Territory, 1879.

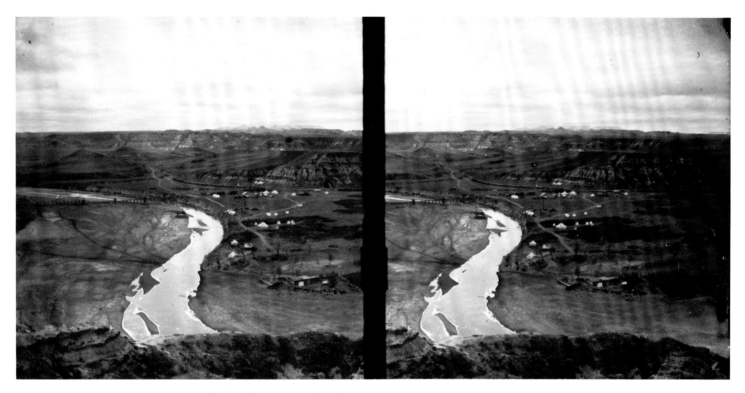

PLATE 61. **Crossing Northern Pacific Railroad, Little Missouri.** Northern Pacific construction camp, and bridge being built across Little Missouri River. West of Medora, Dakota Territory, 1880.

PLATE 62. **Col. Merrill's Quarters, Camp Villard.** Officers of military escort for construction crews, on the Yellowstone River near Billings, Montana Territory, 1882.

PLATE 63. **Grading Eagle Butte.** Track grading for the Northern Pacific along the Yellowstone River, a few miles west of Glendive, Montana Territory, 1881.

PLATE 64. **Engineers' Camp, Bozeman Tunnel.** Survey crew involved in construction of the 3610-foot Bozeman Pass tunnel, Montana Territory, 1882.

PLATE 65. **Multnomah Fall, O. R. & N.** Along the route of Oregon Railway and Navigation Company railroad, connecting line from Northern Pacific railroad at Wallula, Washington Territory to Portland. Villard Party at the 620-foot falls, near Portland, 1883.

PLATE 66. **Villard Arch, Fargo.** Arch named in honor of the line's president, Henry Villard, greets the passengers of Northern Pacific railroad's special excursion train en route to the last spike ceremony in Montana, as they pass through Dakota Territory, 1883.

PLATE 67. Completed Northern Pacific tracks at Eagle Butte along the Yellowstone River, Montana, 1894.

PLATE 68. Northern Pacific locomotive with the Haynes Palace Studio Car. Men identified as:
W. A. Finney, W. M. Johnson (engineer), D. J. Moinihan (fireman), E. P. Murphy, B.
Thompson, P. M. Sullevan. Along the spur to Marysville, Montana Territory, April
1889.

PLATE 69. **The Switchback over the Cascade Range.** Temporary switchback trestles built to carry trains until construction was completed on the Stampede Tunnel in the Cascade Mountains, Washington, 1890.

PLATE 70. Butte Short Line railway trestle in the Silver Bow Valley near Pipestone Pass, Montana, August 1890.

PLATE 71. Engineer D. H. Driscoll and crew pose with Northern Pacific locomotive No. 128, near Glendive, Montana Territory, July 1889.

PLATE 72. Northern Pacific locomotive No. 140 at water tower near Livingston, Montana
     Territory, November 5, 1886.

PLATE 73. **Rotary Snow Plow, N.D.** Track-clearing equipment at unspecified Dakota
Territory location, late 1887.

PLATE 74. In the background, a rotary snow plow approaches. The photographer's view is
        over a snow-cut widener mounted on another locomotive. In the Cascade
        Mountains east of Tacoma, Washington, March 20, 1890.

PLATE 75. Northern Pacific depot, with Mt. Helena in background, at Helena, Montana
Territory, December 1885.

PLATE 76. A Northern Pacific depot and section gang identified as the "A. A. Brownell group,"
Grand Rapids, North Dakota, November 9, 1889.

PLATE 77. Workers pose with engine No. 190 at Northern Pacific repair shops, Sprague, Washington Territory, April 28, 1887.

PLATE 78. Northern Pacific engine No. 196 at brick roundhouse, Glendive, Montana Territory, May 1887.

PLATE 79. Along the Northern Pacific branch line about 100 miles west of Spokane, a crowd poses at Coulee City, Washington, March 1892.

PLATE 80. Northern Pacific railyard with Tacoma city hall and the railroad's own offices in the background, Tacoma, Washington, 1894.

PLATE 81. Cigar counter, registration desk, and train ticket counter in the Ryan Hotel lobby, St. Paul, Minnesota, June 27, 1899.

PLATE 82. Barber shop of the Hotel Tacoma, Tacoma, Washington, 1890.

106

PLATE 83. Haynes photographs, along with farm produce, mineral samples, and stuffed
wildlife inside emigration-promoting Northern Pacific exhibition car, 1895.

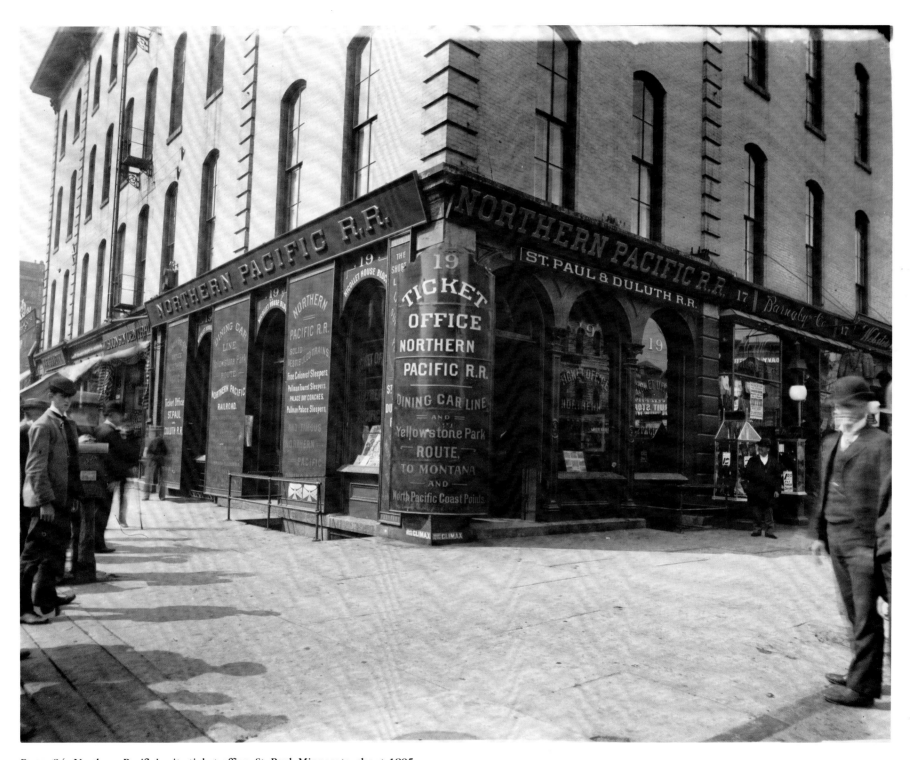

PLATE 84. Northern Pacific's city ticket office, St. Paul, Minnesota, about 1895.

Recording Life in the West

Legislation signed by President Abraham Lincoln on July 2, 1864, created the Northern Pacific Railroad Company and established a land-grant incentive for its construction, providing ten sections of the public domain in the states (Minnesota), and twenty sections in the territories (Dakota, Montana, Idaho, Washington) for each mile of completed track. From this legislation the Northern Pacific ultimately realized more than fifty million acres of land, located in odd-numbered sections on either side of the track. The N.P. continuously attempted to draw investment capital and emigrants into these lands because increased settlement and business activity in the West meant more traffic on the N.P.'s main and branch lines.

F. Jay Haynes, as the Northern Pacific's commissioned photographer from 1876 to 1905, supplied photographs used by the railroad to encourage the expansion of western industry and settlement. These photographs comprise a record of a rapidly changing West — a West that exhibited contrasts of frontier settlement and transplanted Midwestern urbanity. For twenty years (1885-1905), the photographers of the Haynes Palace Studio Car captured the details and diversity of trackside development and life in the West.

Northern Pacific promotional literature attempted to convince the prospective settler/investor that, while there was great opportunity in the untamed American West, there was no need to sacrifice either personal safety or culture to join the westward migration. Thus, many of Haynes' photographs depicted successful commercial ventures that relied on the West's natural resources, while other views emphasized how safe western living had become, following the arrival of the railroad, the depletion of threatening wildlife, and the "civilization" of the native inhabitants.

Haynes also documented the emergence of a distinct western culture: the commercial districts of St. Paul, Helena, and Seattle; the presence of city parks, community parades, and clubs; the amenities of home living. Particularly notable are examples of leisure-time activities and of eastern architecture transferred to western settings. Only indirectly does the Haynes record of life in the West indicate the Northern Pacific's role in this development, but his choice of subjects and skillful composition of views enhanced the N.P.'s ability to lure people and capital to the great Northwest.

PLATE 85. Looking North along 4th Street from the Globe Building, St. Paul, Minnesota, about
1890.

PLATE 86. The photographer's family at their St. Paul home, May 18, 1897. Lily Snyder Haynes
stands on the porch; the children are, from left, George O. Haynes (with bicycle),
Jack E. Haynes near dog, and Bessie Loa Haynes (with bicycle).

PLATE 87. Como Park, St. Paul, Minnesota, August 27, 1896.

PLATE 88. Rice Park, St. Paul, Minnesota, about 1890.

PLATE 89. The racing group of the St. Paul Skating Club pose in Haynes' St. Paul studio, circa 1890.

PLATE 90. Rev. M. D. Edwards, pastor of the Dayton Avenue Presbyterian Church, St. Paul, and his family. Haynes' St. Paul studio, March 31, 1897.

1339 C HALF-BREED BUFFALO BONE PICKERS.

PLATE 91. **Buffalo Bone Pickers, Halfbreeds and Red River Carts.** Bones gleaned from the plains were being sold by weight by the time Haynes took this photo at Minnewaukan, Dakota Territory, May 24, 1886.

PLATE 92. The interior of Allen's taxidermy store, Mandan, North Dakota, 1894.

1392 C MAIN STREET, CARRINGTON, D. T.

PLATE 93. The main street of Carrington, Dakota Territory, with Hotel McKay in foreground,
May 24, 1886.

PLATE 94. Looking west from the Evans hotel's veranda, Hot Springs, South Dakota, 1892.

PLATE 95. The Homestake Mine at Lead, in the Black Hills of South Dakota, 1892.

PLATE 96. The employees and plant of the Gull River Lumber Company, Gull River, Minnesota, April 1888.

PLATE 97. Interior view of George N. Smith's log residence at Huntley, Montana Territory, 1881.

PLATE 98. The Smith & Hagy store at Huntley, Montana Territory, 1881.

PLATE 99. Big Timber, Montana Territory, looking toward the Northern Pacific Railroad depot, November 15, 1886.

PLATE 100. The Helena, Montana, business district, looking south along Main Street from the Sixth Avenue intersection, 1894.

3840 FLATHEAD INDIAN AGENCY
HAYNES-PHOTO.

PLATE 101. **Flathead Indian Agency.** Agency employees and their families, Montana Territory, 1884.

PLATE 102. Cowboys and cattle herd on eastern Montana rangeland, near Miles City, 1894.

PLATE 103. The Haynes Palace Studio Car appears in the right foreground of this view of Potter
& Chandler's mining and smelting operation at Wickes, Montana Territory,
December 1886.

PLATE 104. Potter & Chandler charcoal kilns, Wickes, Montana Territory, December 1886.

PLATE 105. Northern Pacific locomotive No. 334 in front of Lakeside House, Hope, Idaho, 1891.

PLATE 106. Interior of Bach Cory & Co. dry goods store at Gregory, Montana Territory, December 1886.

PLATE 107. **Salmon Fishing, Columbia River.** Near the cascades of the Columbia River, Oregon, 1885.

PLATE 108. A giant cedar in the Chehalis Valley, Washington, August 1890.

PLATE 109. Residence of Col. Howlit, Yakima, Washington, August 1890.

PLATE 110. Unidentified residence, Cowlitz Valley of Washington, August 1890.

PLATE 111. **Loading Colliers, Seattle.** Unidentified steamer is being loaded at right, steamer *Willamette* in center, 1890.

PLATE 112. Following a major fire in 1889, reconstruction along Yessler Avenue, Seattle, Washington, spring 1890.

In Yellow Stone Country

Five years after Congress created Yellowstone National Park in 1872, the nation's first such park, F. Jay Haynes wanted to visit "the Yellow Stone Country," but he did not see the Park until 1881. The Northern Pacific Railroad commissioned him, in that year, to produce photographs of Yellowstone's natural wonders to be used in promoting tourist travel. For four decades, Haynes annually returned to the Park until his death in 1921.

Haynes' first trip to Yellowstone changed his life. As a photographer committed to the recording of artistic views, he had always sought grand views and nature's unique works as subjects. In the "Wonderland's" geological features he discovered a concentration of these, unparalleled in the American West. Haynes dedicated a major portion of his commercial future to photographing Yellowstone. In 1881 he applied to the Department of the Interior for permission to locate in the Park; in 1884 he became a Yellowstone concessionaire, a franchise he held until relinquishing the business to his son in 1916. The greatest fame of F. Jay Haynes has derived from his photographs of this "Wonderland," from Old Faithful Geyser to little known natural features, and his two winter trips, in 1887 and 1894, that allowed him to set Yellowstone's sights in an even more dramatic context.

In many ways, the story of the early national parks is the story of transporting and accommodating the tourist. Because of his commercial interests in the Park, Haynes' views document the development of transportation systems and the construction of magnificent seasonal hotels, where he eventually located photo stands. Many of his photos included tourists, demonstrating the accessibility of the Park's attractions.

At a time when photographic equipment was heavy and bulky, the photographer and his assistants clambered over the Park's rugged terrain to select precise locations from which memorable scenes could be recorded. Through his various outlets in Yellowstone — including the landmark Haynes Studio at Mammoth Hot Springs — Haynes provided distinctive photographic views with which the tourist could commemorate his stay in the "Wonderland."

For more than thirty years F. Jay Haynes served as the "Official Photographer of Yellowstone National Park." In this position he created an extensive record of the Park's natural features and of its human modifications. Moreover Haynes loved the Park and, on several levels, contributed to its popularity and development. His photographs of the Park reflect Haynes' interpretation of the enabling legislation, where it defines Yellowstone as "a public park or pleasureing-ground [*sic*] dedicated and set apart for the benefit and enjoyment of the people," and they also reflect his growth as a landscape photographer of great ability.

PLATE 113. **Our Artist Bound for the Canyon.** F. Jay Haynes, at right, with photographic equipment on sledge in Yellowstone National Park, 1887.

PLATE 114. **Golden Gate and Pillar, West Gardner.** Road construction in Yellowstone, 1884.

PLATE 115: Interior, during construction, of the National Hotel at Mammoth Hot Springs, Yellowstone, 1883.

PLATE 116. **Interior Mammoth Cave, South End.** Tourists explore underground in the
Devil's Kitchen area near Mammoth Hot Springs, 1884.

PLATE 117. **Veranda, Hotel Norris.** The hotel built in autumn 1886 by the Yellowstone
Park Association, as photographed in January 1887.

PLATE 118. **Great Falls from Red Rock.** View toward the Grand Canyon of the
Yellowstone River, January 1887.

PLATE 119. **Up the Basin from the Castle.** Castle Geyser, left, in the Upper Geyser Basin, January 1887.

PLATE 120. **The Riverside Geyser.** Upper Geyser Basin, Firehole River at left, 1896.

PLATE 121. Bicyclists pause at Old Faithful Geyser, September 15, 1895.

PLATE 122. Giant Geyser in the Upper Geyser Basin, 1899.

PLATE 123. Tourist stagecoaches prepare to leave the Mammoth Hot Springs area, 1896.

PLATE 124. Tourists view the Lower Falls of the Yellowstone River from its brink, 1886.

PLATE 125. Tourist camping party at the foot of Jupiter Terrace, Mammoth Hot Springs area, July 29, 1891.

PLATE 126. Norris Lunch Station employees pose with their catch; background tents comprise
the Station, owned by Lawrence Francis Mathews (seated), 1896.

PLATE 127. View from Capitol Hill toward Mt. Everts, showing Fort Yellowstone installation of
U.S. Army, which then administered the Park, in 1895.

PLATE 128. Mammoth Hot Springs valley from Mound Terrace, about 1895.

PLATE 129. The then recently-completed Old Faithful Inn, with Jack Ellis Haynes in foreground, 1904.

PLATE 130. Lobby of Old Faithful Inn, 1904.

PLATE 131. Souvenir Yellowstone views are displayed at Haynes' first sales stand in the National Hotel lobby, Mammoth Hot Springs, 1896.

PLATE 132. Elk graze inside the elkhorn fence of the Haynes studio (and summertime family residence) at Mammoth Hot Springs, 1898.

PLATE 133. Fountain Paint Pot, 1895.

PLATE 134. Narrow Gauge Terrace, 1896.

PLATE 135. Gibbon Falls, 1888.

PLATE 136. **Tower Falls and Canyon.** 1883.

PLATE 137. **Yellowstone Lake, West Thumb.** Taken from Rock Cave, October 1889.

PLATE 138. Obsidian Cliff, Beaver Lake, 1899.

PLATE 139. Jupiter Terrace and its reflection, 1899.

PLATE 140. Pulpit and Jupiter Terraces, 1899.

Haynes' Vision of the Landscape

The reputation of F. Jay Haynes derives from his work as a documentary photographer, but his extensive array of documentary views is complemented by his portrait and landscape photography. Although little of the portraiture is extant, a much more representative selection of the landscape work has survived. In some instances, Haynes combined the available landscape with the specific subject required by his contractors. But in other cases — from South Dakota to Alaska to Yellowstone National Park — he concentrated solely on the landscape as an esthetic subject.

Landscape photography in North America developed after 1865 on the basis of two factors: technological advances in supplies, and increased public interest in the natural scene as an artistic subject. As the American public's evolving concept of nature brought increased interest in landscape photography (and easterners were especially curious about western landforms), photographers found new freedoms of travel and work in the field. The wet-collodion negative process was more portable than the daguerrotype, and the albumen paper that replaced salted printing paper allowed for clearer, more detailed prints.

F. Jay Haynes participated in these changes, both by taking advantage of more portable equipment and by taking landscape views that were alternately informative and esthetically pleasing. In his landscape work, although he both embraced and avoided photographic conventions of the day, he experimented.

Haynes constantly experimented with the effects of light in photography, especially in his many photographs of the Grand Canyon of the Yellowstone River. Taking more than one hundred views of the Canyon between 1881 and 1900, in all seasons and at all hours of the day, Haynes sensitively experimented with subtle changes in light as he viewed the Canyon from different standpoints. He purposefully produced many of these views in stereo or in mammoth size (20x24). Because both formats impress the viewer with an image larger than one's field of vision, they thereby approximate the experience of personally beholding the Canyon.

Haynes learned photography by making portraits and stereographs. His concerns in creating these kinds of prints — controlled lighting, strong diagonal elements, phased depth, carefully delineated space — extend into his landscape photographs. He remained remarkably eclectic in spatial interpretation.

In these photographic studies, Haynes evinced the extensive vocabulary that he commanded and continued to apply in composition and in the use of light, as he expressed his esthetic vision of the western landscape.

PLATE 141. **Turk's Head, Satan's Wall.** Missouri River in background, summer 1880.

PLATE 142. **Summit of the Glacier, Mission Range.** Subject poses on a snowfield in the
Mission Mountain Range, Montana Territory, 1884.

PLATE 143. **Thompson Falls and City, M.T.** The settlement that came to be called
Thompson Falls, as photographed in Montana Territory, 1884.

PLATE 144. **Soda Butte Spring and Valley.** In Yellowstone National Park, 1884.

PLATE 145. **Palisades, Columbia River.** Oregon, 1885.

PLATE 146. **Brink of Snoqualmie Falls.** East of Seattle, spring 1890.

PLATE 147. **Cabinet Gorge, Clark's Forks River.** The Clark Fork of the Columbia River, Montana, about 1889.

PLATE 148. **The Beautiful Pools of the Green River.** Pools along the Green River south
of Seattle, August 1890.

PLATE 149. Sioux Pass in the Black Hills, near Hot Springs, South Dakota, 1892.

PLATE 150. Sylvan Lake near Hill City, South Dakota, 1892.

PLATE 151. **The Pillar of Hercules and Columbia River.** Tracks of the Oregon River &
Navigation Road (a Northern Pacific branch-line) parallel the river east of Portland,
Oregon, and run between the Pillars of Hercules, 1885.

PLATE 152. **Oneonta Gorge, Oregon.** Along the Columbia River, 1885.

PLATE 153. **Crater Rock, Mt. Tacoma.** Ice fields on the peak now known as Mt. Rainier, Washington, 1889.

3908 ABOVE THE CLOUDS FROM MT. TACOMA

HAYNES-PHOTO.

PLATE 154. **Above the Clouds from Mt. Tacoma.** The top of a cloud bank on Mt. Rainier, Washington, 1890.

PLATE 155. Seward Webb Glacier, Teton Mountains, Wyoming, September 1896.

PLATE 156. Bluff overlooking site of Billings, Montana, 1894.

PLATE 157. Along the shore of Lake Pend d'Oreille, Idaho, August 1890.

PLATE 158. **Taku Glacier.** Glacier and ice floes, Alaska, 1891.

PLATE 159. Grand Canyon of the Yellowstone River, Yellowstone National Park, downstream from the falls, 1899.

PLATE 160. Lower Falls of the Yellowstone River, Yellowstone National Park, taken from Red Rock, 1899.

Note on Research Materials

Biographical information on F. Jay Haynes in this book is based upon research in two major collections of primary materials: the Yellowstone National Park and Manuscript Collection (the Haynes Book and Manuscript Collection), held by the Special Collections Division of the Montana State University Library, Bozeman, and the F. Jay Haynes Photographic Studio Collection materials, held by the Montana Historical Society Archives in Helena.

Jack Ellis Haynes assembled both collections from the family's business and personal records, as well as from supplemental sources. These manuscript and printed materials document the life of F. Jay Haynes, the members of his immediate family, and the "House of Haynes," which operated in Yellowstone National Park for more than eighty-five years. Isabel M. Haynes, widow of Jack Ellis Haynes, donated the collections to the two repositories in the name of the Haynes family.

The Haynes Book and Manuscript Collection, in Special Collections, Montana State University Library, includes more than ten thousand pamphlets, articles, and books dealing particularly with Montana history and Yellowstone National Park, F. Jay Haynes' personal and family correspondence (1873-1921) and various personal writings of several family members. In addition, this collection includes exhaustive business correspondence and records, covering business operations from 1876 to 1917, from Moorhead, Minnesota to Mammoth Hot Springs. Also helpful are articles written by Jack Ellis Haynes, his "Haynes Bulletin" newsletter, and the sixty-four-edition *Haynes Guide to Yellowstone National Park* (1890-1964).

The F. Jay Haynes Photographic Studio Collections materials, housed in the Montana Historical Society Archives, comprise manuscripts and records that document the Haynes Photograph Collection of more than 23,500 photographs. These materials include photographic notebooks, studio portrait registers, merchandise order books, and Haynes Palace Studio Car ledgers (1885-1906).

Reference List of Illustrations

A short title is listed here for each numbered plate, and each illustration in the introductory text. "N.P." refers to Northern Pacific Railroad. "YNP" refers to Yellowstone National Park. Date given is that of original negative. Height precedes width in dimensions of negative. If image from original was altered for this book, the entry notes whether "cropped" or "reduced." Montana Historical Society-assigned number for each image completes the entry.

p. 7   F. JAY HAYNES, 1875.
Photographer unknown. Uncased tintype, 3⅝x2⅝".

p. 8   LOCKWOOD'S MODEL GALLERY, 1875.
Photographer unknown. Cropped half stereo view, 4x7".

p. 9   LOCKWOOD'S GALLERY, RIPON, WISCONSIN, 1875.
top   Photographer unknown. Cropped half stereo view, 4x7".

p. 9   HAYNES' FIRST MOORHEAD, MINN. GALLERY, 1876.
bottom   Cropped half stereo view from 5x8" wet plate neg. #H-3

p. 10   LILY SNYDER HAYNES AND F. JAY HAYNES, 1878.
8x5" wet plate neg. #H-4277

p. 11   F. JAY HAYNES AT FIREHOLE RIVER, YNP, 1883.
Haynes Studio. 8x10" dry plate neg. (cropped) #H-970

p. 12   F. JAY HAYNES, 1882.
top   Haynes Studio. 5x4" dry plate neg. (cropped) #H-742

p. 12   HAYNES' MAMMOTH HOT SPRINGS STUDIO, YNP,
bottom   1884.
8x10" dry plate neg. (cropped) #H-3726

p. 13   HAYNES PALACE STUDIO CAR, INTERIOR, 1886.
top   8x10" dry plate neg. (cropped) #H-1797

p. 13   HAYNES PALACE STUDIO CAR, EXTERIOR, 1901.
bottom   8x10" dry plate neg. (cropped) #H-3997

p. 14   HAYNES PALACE STUDIO CAR POSTER, 1890.
26x11" red & black poster (loc. unk.) #H-61017

p. 15   HAYNES SALES COUNTER, NATIONAL HOTEL, YNP, 1892.
8x10" dry plate neg. #H-2687

p. 16   HAYNES ST. PAUL STUDIO INTERIOR, 1893.
8x10" dry plate neg. (cropped) #H-2991

p. 17   JACK E. HAYNES, 1918.
right   8x5" dry plate neg. (cropped) #H-18001A

p. 17   F. JAY HAYNES AND FAMILY, 1913.
left   5x8" dry plate neg. #H-4380

PLATES

1. DEPOT, BISMARCK, D.T., 1877.
5x8" wet plate stereo neg., #H-68.

2. TIMES OFFICE, FARGO, D.T., 1876.
5x8" wet plate stereo neg., #H-7.

3. UNION SCHOOL, FARGO, D.T., 1878.
5x8" wet plate stereo neg., #H-191.

4. SOUTHWEST FROM HEADQUARTERS HOTEL, FARGO, D.T., 1876.
5x8" wet plate stereo neg., #H-21.

5. J. A. JOHNSON & CO.'S STEAM THRESHER, FARGO, D.T., 1881.
5x8" dry plate neg., #H-108.

6. MAIN STREET, MOORHEAD, MINN., 1876.
5x8" wet plate stereo neg., #H-14.

7. BARNES RESIDENCE, FARGO, D.T., 1883.
5x8" wet plate stereo neg. (cropped), #H-903.

8. E. A. GRANT'S STORE, FARGO, D.T., 1876.
5x8" wet plate stereo neg., #H-17.

9. BESSIE LOA HAYNES, 1883.
8x5" dry plate neg., #H-1261.

10. LILY SNYDER HAYNES, 1880.
8x5" wet plate neg., #H-4285.

11. PLOW TEAMS, SPIRITWOOD FARMS, 1880.
5x8" dry plate stereo neg. (cropped), #H-267.

12. PRAIRIE BREAKING, DALRYMPLE FARM, 1878.
5x8" wet plate stereo neg. (cropped), #H-192.

13. SELF-BINDERS, WILLIAMS FARM, 1878.
5x8" wet plate neg. (cropped), #H-202.

14. THRESHING IN RED RIVER VALLEY, 1878.
5x8" wet plate neg., #H-215.

15. FARM HANDS, BARNES FARM, 1879.
5x8" wet plate neg., #H-238.

16. PRESIDENTIAL EXCURSION PARTY, 1878.
5x8" wet plate neg., #H-203.

17. FLAT BOAT BUILDING, RED RIVER, 1876.
5x8" wet plate stereo neg. (cropped), #H-13.

18. UNION GRAIN ELEVATOR, FARGO, D.T., 1881.
5x8" dry plate neg., #H-105.

19. STEAMER SELKIRK, 1877.
5x8" wet plate stereo neg. (cropped), #H-77.

20. BISMARCK LEVEE, 1877.
    5x8" wet plate stereo neg., #H-58.
21. RED RIVER FLOOD, 1881.
    5x8" dry plate neg., #H-111.
22. MISSOURI RIVER ICE BREAKUP, 1881.
    5x8" dry plate stereo neg. (cropped), #H-432.
23. CITY OF WORCESTER, 1878.
    5x8" wet plate stereo neg. (cropped), #H-209.
24. CITY OF WORCESTER, INTERIOR, 1878.
    5x8" wet plate stereo neg., #H-207.
25. INDIAN VILLAGE NORTH OF CITY, 1877.
    5x8" wet plate stereo neg. (cropped), #H-78.
26. MEDICINE MAN, YELLOW DOG, AND SQUAWS, 1883.
    8x5" dry plate neg. (cropped), #H-1059.
27. BIG MEDICINE MAN, 1883.
    8x5" dry plate neg. (cropped), #H-949.
28. YELLOW DOG, 1883.
    8x5" dry plate neg. (cropped), #H-947.
29. WALL ST., DEADWOOD, D.T., 1877.
    5x8" dry plate neg., #H-119.
30. BLACK TAIL GULCH, 1877.
    5x8" wet plate stereo neg. (cropped), #H-157.
31. SIGNAL HILL, CENTRAL, D.T., 1877.
    5x8" wet plate stereo neg., #H-132.
32. OUR ARTIST AT THE FALLS, 1880.
    5x8" dry plate stereo neg. (cropped), #H-323.
33. LANDING, COW ISLAND, M.T., 1880.
    5x8" dry plate stereo neg. (cropped), #H-318.
34. FORT BENTON, FROM BLUFFS, 1880.
    5x8" dry plate stereo neg. (cropped), #H-331.
35. FIRST VIEW OF THE BAD LANDS, 1880.
    5x8" dry plate stereo neg. (cropped), #H-280.
36. "WOODING UP" IN THE MOUNTAINS, 1880.
    5x8" dry plate stereo neg. (cropped), #H-342.
37. MISSION SCHOOL, DEVILS LAKE AGENCY, D.T., 1881.
    5x8" dry plate neg., #H-572.
38. GATTLING GUN BATTERY, FORT TOTTEN, D.T., 1881.
    5x8" dry plate stereo neg. (cropped), #H-593.
39. STEAM SHOVEL AND SAND PIT, 1881.
    5x8" dry plate stereo neg., #H-522.
40. HUDSON'S BAY CO.'S POST, RAT PORTAGE, 1881.
    5x8" dry plate stereo neg., #H-497.
41. LUMBER YARD, KEEWATIN MILLS, 1881.
    5x8" dry plate stereo neg., #H-510.
42. LOG BOOM, KEEWATIN MILLS, 1881.
    5x8" dry plate stereo neg., #H-508.
43. HAYNES' WAGON IN LOWER CANYON OF THE YELLOWSTONE, YNP, 1881.
    5x8" dry plate stereo neg. (cropped), #H-681.
44. GRAND CANYON OF THE YELLOWSTONE, 1881.
    5x8" dry plate stereo neg. (cropped), #H-675.
45. LONE STAR GEYSER CONE, YNP, 1882.
    5x8" dry plate stereo neg. (cropped), #H-797.
46. GEYSER IMMEDIATELY AFTER ERUPTION, YNP, 1881.
    5x8" dry plate stereo neg., #H-642.
47. PRESIDENTIAL PARTY AT UPPER GEYSER BASIN, 1883.
    8x10" dry plate neg., #H-1052.
48. ARAPAHOE INDIAN CHIEFS, FORT WASHAKIE, 1883.
    8x10" dry plate neg., #H-1013.
49. CREVASSE IN MUIR GLACIER, 1891.
    8x10" dry plate neg. (cropped), #H-2594.

50. STR. "QUEEN" APPROACHING MUIR GLACIER, 1891.
    8x10" dry plate neg., #H-2581.
51. THE WHALE, FORT WRANGELL, 1891.
    8x10" dry plate neg., #H-2546.
52. JUNEAU, ALASKA, 1891.
    8x10" dry plate neg., #H-2569.
53. W. S. WEBB EXCURSION CAMP, 1896.
    8x10" dry plate neg., #H-3658.
54. W. S. WEBB AND GUIDE BAPTISTE, 1896.
    8x10" dry plate neg., #H-3662.
55. LOADING N.P. TRANSFER, BISMARCK, D.T., 1880.
    5x8" dry plate stereo neg. (cropped), #H-278.
56. UP THE MISSOURI FROM LEVEE, BISMARCK, D.T., 1876.
    5x8" wet plate stereo neg., #H-44.
57. CONSTRUCTION OF THE N.P. BRIDGE, BISMARCK, D.T., 1881.
    5x8" dry plate stereo neg. (cropped), #H-426.
58. TESTING THE BISMARCK BRIDGE, 1882.
    5x8" dry plate neg. (cropped), #H-812.
59. EAST ENTRANCE TO MULLAN TUNNEL, 1883.
    5x8" dry plate stereo neg. (cropped), #H-1092.
60. BIG CUT AND SWEET BRIAR VALLEY, 1879.
    5x8" wet plate stereo neg., #H-228.
61. CROSSING N.P.R.R., LITTLE MISSOURI, D.T., 1880.
    5x8" dry plate stereo neg. (cropped), #H-301.
62. COL. MERRILL'S QUARTERS, CAMP VILLARD, 1882.
    5x8" dry plate stereo neg. (cropped), #H-747.
63. GRADING EAGLE BUTTE, 1881.
    5x8" dry plate stereo neg. (cropped), #H-711.
64. ENGINEERS' CAMP, BOZEMAN TUNNEL, 1882.
    5x8" dry plate stereo neg. (cropped), #H-749.
65. MULTNOMAH FALLS, VILLARD PARTY, 1883.
    10x8" dry plate neg. (reduced), #H-1001.
66. VILLARD ARCH, FARGO, D.T., 1883.
    8x10" dry plate neg., #H-974.
67. N.P. TRACKS, EAGLE BUTTE, MONTANA, 1894.
    8x10" dry plate neg., #H-3112.
68. N.P. LOCOMOTIVE WITH HAYNES PALACE STUDIO CAR, 1889.
    8x10" dry plate neg., #H-2045.
69. SWITCHBACK OVER THE CASCADE RANGE, 1890.
    8x10" dry plate neg. (cropped), #H-2215.
70. BUTTE SHORT LINE TRESTLE, M.T., 1890.
    8x10" dry plate neg., #H-2335.
71. LOCOMOTIVE NO. 128, NEAR GLENDIVE, M.T., 1889.
    8x10" dry plate neg., #H-2051.
72. N.P. LOCOMOTIVE NO. 140 AT WATER TOWER, 1886.
    8x10" dry plate neg., #H-1715.
73. ROTARY SNOW PLOW, D.T., 1887.
    8x10" dry plate neg. (cropped), #H-1801.
74. ROTARY SNOW PLOW AND SNOW CUT WIDENER, 1890.
    8x10" dry plate neg. (cropped), #H-2378.
75. N.P. DEPOT, HELENA, M.T., 1885.
    8x10" dry plate neg., #H-1570.
76. N.P. DEPOT AND SECTION GANG, GRAND RAPIDS, N.D., 1889.
    8x10" dry plate neg., #H-2052.
77. WORKERS AND REPAIR SHOPS, SPRAGUE, WASHINGTON TERR., 1887.
    8x10" dry plate neg. (cropped), #H-1811.

78. ROUNDHOUSE, GLENDIVE, M.T., 1887.
    8x10" dry plate neg. (cropped), #H-1822.
79. COULEE CITY, WASHINGTON, 1892.
    8x10" dry plate neg., #H-2694.
80. N.P. RAILYARD, TACOMA, WASHINGTON, 1894.
    8x10" dry plate neg., #H-3249.
81. RYAN HOTEL LOBBY, ST. PAUL, MINNESOTA, 1899.
    8x10" dry plate neg., #H-3816.
82. BARBER SHOP, HOTEL TACOMA, 1890.
    8x10" dry plate neg., #H-2232.
83. N.P. EXHIBITION CAR, 1895.
    8x10" dry plate neg., #H-3311.
84. N.P. TICKET OFFICE, ST. PAUL, MINNESOTA, 1895.
    8x10" dry plate neg., #H-4715.
85. ST. PAUL, MINNESOTA, 1890.
    8x10" dry plate neg. (cropped), #H-2415.
86. HAYNES FAMILY AT THEIR ST. PAUL HOME, 1897.
    8x10" dry plate neg., #H-3690.
87. COMO PARK, ST. PAUL, MINNESOTA, 1896.
    8x10" dry plate neg., #H-3555.
88. RICE PARK, ST. PAUL, MINNESOTA, 1890.
    8x10" dry plate neg. (cropped), #H-2439.
89. ST. PAUL SKATING CLUB, 1890.
    8x10" dry plate neg., #H-4719.
90. REV. M. D. EDWARDS, AND FAMILY, 1897.
    8x10" dry plate neg. (cropped), #H-3688.
91. BUFFALO BONE PICKERS, 1886.
    8x10" dry plate neg. (cropped), #H-1702.
92. ALLEN'S TAXIDERMY STORE, MANDAN, N.D., 1894.
    8x10" dry plate neg., #H-3090.
93. CARRINGTON, DAKOTA TERRITORY, 1886.
    8x10" dry plate neg. (cropped), #H-1703.
94. EVANS HOTEL, HOT SPRINGS, SOUTH DAKOTA, 1892.
    8x10" dry plate neg., #H-2854.
95. HOMESTAKE MINE, LEAD, SOUTH DAKOTA, 1892.
    8x10" dry plate neg. (cropped), #H-2928.
96. GULL RIVER LUMBER COMPANY, MINNESOTA, 1888.
    8x10" dry plate neg., #H-1920.
97. SMITH'S RESIDENCE, HUNTLEY, M.T., 1881.
    5x8" dry plate stereo neg., #H-559.
98. SMITH & HAGY STORE, HUNTLEY, M.T., 1881.
    5x8" dry plate neg., #H-558.
99. BIG TIMBER, MONTANA TERRITORY, 1886.
    8x10" dry plate neg., #H-1718.
100. HELENA, MONTANA, 1894.
    8x10" dry plate neg., #H-3192.
101. FLATHEAD INDIAN AGENCY, M.T., 1884.
    8x10" dry plate neg. (cropped), #H-2007.
102. COWBOYS AND CATTLE HERD, 1894.
    8x10" dry plate neg., #H-3118.
103. WICKES, MONTANA TERRITORY, 1886.
    8x10" dry plate neg., #H-1746.
104. CHARCOAL KILNS, WICKES, M.T., 1886.
    8x10" dry plate neg. (cropped), #H-1749.
105. N.P. LOCOMOTIVE #334, HOPE, IDAHO, 1891.
    8x10" dry plate neg., #H-2632.
106. BACH CORY STORE, GREGORY, M.T., 1886.
    8x10" dry plate neg., #H-1748.
107. SALMON FISHING, COLUMBIA RIVER, 1885.
    8x10" dry plate neg. (cropped), #H-1673.

108. GIANT CEDAR, CHEHALIS VALLEY, WASHINGTON, 1890.
8x10" dry plate neg., #H-2096.

109. HOWLIT RESIDENCE, YAKIMA, WASHINGTON, 1890.
8x10" dry plate neg., #H-2113.

110. RESIDENCE, COWLITZ VALLEY, WASHINGTON, 1890.
8x10" dry plate neg., #H-2095.

111. LOADING COLLIERS, SEATTLE, WASHINGTON, 1890.
8x10" dry plate neg., #H-2250.

112. YESSLER AVENUE, SEATTLE, WASHINGTON, 1890.
8x10" dry plate neg., #H-2255.

113. OUR ARTIST BOUND FOR THE CANYON, 1887.
5x8" dry plate stereo neg., #H-1845.

114. GOLDEN GATE AND PILLAR, YNP, 1884.
5x8" dry plate stereo neg. (cropped), #H-1315.

115. NATIONAL HOTEL DURING CONSTRUCTION, YNP, 1883.
5x8" dry plate stereo neg. (cropped), #H-877.

116. INTERIOR, MAMMOTH CAVE, YNP, 1884.
5x8" dry plate stereo neg. (cropped), #H-1305.

117. VERANDA, HOTEL NORRIS, YNP, 1887.
8x10" dry plate neg. (cropped), #H-1853.

118. GREAT FALLS FROM RED ROCK, YNP, 1887.
8x10" dry plate neg., #H-1893.

119. UP THE BASIN FROM THE CASTLE, YNP, 1887.
8x10" dry plate neg. (cropped), #H-1867.

120. RIVERSIDE GEYSER, YNP, 1896.
8x10" dry plate neg., #H-3668.

121. OLD FAITHFUL GEYSER, YNP, 1895.
10x8" dry plate neg. (reduced), #H-3322.

122. GIANT GEYSER, YNP, 1899.
8x10" dry plate neg., #H-3942.

123. TOURIST STAGECOACHES, YNP, 1896.
8x10" dry plate neg., #H-3605.

124. TOURISTS VIEWING LOWER FALLS, YNP, 1886.
8x10" dry plate neg. (cropped), #H-1776.

125. CAMPING PARTY, JUPITER TERRACE, YNP, 1891.
8x10" dry plate neg. (cropped), #H-2658.

126. NORRIS LUNCH STATION, YNP, 1896.
8x10" dry plate neg., #H-3611.

127. FORT YELLOWSTONE, YNP, 1895.
8x10" dry plate neg., #H-3321.

128. MAMMOTH HOT SPRINGS, YNP, 1895.
8x10" dry plate neg., #H-3341.

129. OLD FAITHFUL INN, EXTERIOR, YNP, 1904.
8x10" dry plate neg., #H-4601.

130. LOBBY OF OLD FAITHFUL INN, YNP, 1904.
8x10" dry plate neg., #H-5201.

131. NATIONAL HOTEL LOBBY, YNP, 1896.
8x10" dry plate neg., #H-3582.

132. HAYNES STUDIO WITH ELKHORN FENCE, YNP, 1898.
8x10" dry plate neg., #H-3762.

133. FOUNTAIN PAINT POT, YNP, 1895.
8x10" dry plate neg., #H-3431.

134. NARROW GAUGE TERRACE, YNP, 1896.
8x10" dry plate neg., #H-3673.

135. GIBBON FALLS, YNP, 1888.
8x10" dry plate neg., #H-1956.

136. TOWER FALL, YNP, 1883.
10x8" dry plate neg. (reduced), #H-968.

137. YELLOWSTONE LAKE, 1889.
8x10" dry plate neg., #H-2002.

138. OBSIDIAN CLIFF, YNP, 1899.
8x10" dry plate neg., #H-3940.

139. JUPITER TERRACE, YNP, 1899.
8x10" dry plate neg., #H-3927.

140. PULPIT AND JUPITER TERRACES, YNP, 1899.
8x10" dry plate neg., #H-3925.

141. TURK'S HEAD, 1880.
5x8" dry plate stereo neg. (cropped), #H-366.

142. SUMMIT OF THE GLACIER, MISSION RANGE, 1884.
5x8" dry plate stereo neg. (cropped), #H-1358.

143. THOMPSON FALLS, M.T., 1884.
5x8" dry plate stereo neg. (cropped), #H-1378.

144. SODA BUTTE SPRING AND VALLEY, YNP, 1884.
5x8" dry plate stereo neg. (cropped), #H-1529.

145. PALISADES, COLUMBIA RIVER, 1885.
8x10" dry plate neg., #H-1642.

146. SNOQUALMIE FALLS, 1890.
8x10" dry plate neg., #H-2285.

147. CABINET GORGE, CLARK FORK RIVER, 1889.
8x10" dry plate neg., #H-2033.

148. GREEN RIVER, 1890.
8x10" dry plate neg., #H-2290.

149. SIOUX PASS, SOUTH DAKOTA, 1892.
8x10" dry plate neg., #H-2880.

150. SYLVAN LAKE, SOUTH DAKOTA, 1892.
8x10" dry plate neg., #H-2942.

151. PILLARS OF HERCULES AND COLUMBIA RIVER, 1885.
8x10" dry plate neg., #H-1659.

152. ONEONTA GORGE, OREGON, 1885.
10x8" dry plate neg. (reduced), #H-1665.

153. CRATER ROCK, MT. TACOMA, 1889.
8x10" dry plate neg. (cropped), #H-2040.

154. ABOVE THE CLOUDS FROM MT. TACOMA, 1890.
8x10" dry plate neg. (cropped), #H-2206.

155. SEWARD WEBB GLACIER, 1896.
8x10" dry plate neg. (cropped), #H-3709.

156. BLUFF OVERLOOKING BILLINGS, MONTANA, 1894.
8x10" dry plate neg., #H-3157.

157. LAKE PEND D'OREILLE, IDAHO, 1890.
8x10" dry plate neg., #H-2296.

158. TAKU GLACIER, 1891.
8x10" dry plate neg., #H-2564.

159. GRAND CANYON OF THE YELLOWSTONE, 1899.
8x10" dry plate neg., #H-3905.

160. LOWER FALLS OF THE YELLOWSTONE, 1899.
8x10" dry plate neg., #H-3903.

F. Jay Haynes, Photographer was designed by William L. Lang and Barbara C. Fifer using contact prints produced directly from Haynes' glass plate negatives by Mary Fleenor. The photographs were reproduced via 200-line screen black on black duotones, on Warren Lustro Offset Enamel paper in cream. Text was composed in Garamond Book by Thurber Printing Company, Helena, Montana. The book was printed and bound by Kingsport Press, Kingsport, Tennessee.